SMOKEJUMPER:
12 THINGS TO KNOW

by Samantha S. Bell

STORY LIBRARY
MORE TO EXPLORE

www.12StoryLibrary.com

12-Story Library is an imprint of Bookstaves.

Developed and produced for 12-Story Library by Focus Strategic Communications Inc.

Library of Congress Cataloging-in-Publication Data
Names: Bell, Samantha, author.
Title: Smokejumper : 12 things to know / by Samantha S. Bell.
Description: Mankato, Minnesota : 12-Story Library, [2022] | Series: Daring and dangerous jobs | Includes bibliographical references and index. | Audience: Ages 10–13. | Audience: Grades 4–6.
Identifiers: LCCN 2020018548 (print) | LCCN 2020018549 (ebook) | ISBN 9781632359445 (library binding) | ISBN 9781632359797 (paperback) | ISBN 9781645821090 (pdf)
Subjects: LCSH: Smokejumpers—Juvenile literature. | Smokejumping—Vocational guidance—Juvenile literature.
Classification: LCC SD421.23 .B455 2022 (print) | LCC SD421.23 (ebook) | DDC 634.9/618—dc23
LC record available at https://lccn.loc.gov/2020018548
LC ebook record available at https://lccn.loc.gov/2020018549

Photographs ©: forestproud/YouTube.com, cover, 1; U.S. Forest Service/USDA/Peter Buschmann, 4; agefotostock/Alamy, 5; PBH/Alamy, 5; U.S. Forest Service – Pacific Northwest Region, 6; U.S. Bureau of Land Management/NIFC/CC2.0, 7; USDA Photo/Alamy, 7; Ami Vitale/Alamy, 8; U.S. Forest Service/USDA/Lance Cheung, 9; U.S. Forest Service – Pacific Southwest Region 5/CC2.0, 9; Guy Kitchens/ZUMA Press, Inc./Alamy, 10; AB Forces News Collection/Alamy, 11; Ami Vitale/Alamy, 11; National Archives and Records Administration, 12; U.S. Forest Service - Pacific Northwest Region, 13; U.S. Forest Service/USDA/Lance Cheung, 14; Don Despain/Alamy, 15; U.S. Forest Service – Pacific Southwest Region 5/CC2.0, 15; U.S. Forest Service – Pacific Southwest Region 5/CC2.0, 16; Eugene Berman/Shutterstock.com, 16; Joseph Sohm/Shutterstock.com, 17; Christian Roberts-Olsen/Shutterstock.com, 18; Nature and Science/Alamy, 19; U.S. Department of Agriculture/Lance Cheung, 20; U.S. Forest Service/USDA, 21; Tatiana Zinchenko/Shutterstock.com, 21; Ami Vitale/Alamy, 22; Nature and Science/Alamy, 22; U.S. Forest Service – Pacific Southwest Region 5/CC2.0, 23; Kritthaneth/Shutterstock.com, 23; U.S. Department of Agriculture/Lance Cheung, 24; U.S. Forest Service – Pacific Southwest Region 5/CC2.0, 25; Ursa Major/Shutterstock.com, 25; Nature and Science/Alamy, 26; Ami Vitale/Alamy, 26; Ami Vitale/Alamy, 27; USFS Photo/Alamy, 28; Will Seberger/ZUMAPRESS.com/Alamy, 28; George S de Blonsky/Alamy, 29

About the Cover
Naomi Mills is a smokejumper with the US Forest Service.

Access free, up-to-date content on this topic plus a full digital version of this book. Scan the QR code on page 31 or use your school's login at 12StoryLibrary.com.

Table of Contents

1

Smokejumpers Are Professional Firefighters

Wildfires can burn millions of acres of land. They move fast, destroying forests and cities. Firefighters work to put out the wildfires. Some even parachute directly into the fires. They are called *smokejumpers*.

Every year wildfires destroy thousands of acres of forests and vegetation.

A smokejumper's main job is to stop a wildfire from becoming too big. Some areas are so remote that they cannot be reached by road. Smokejumpers go into these areas. They often remain there for days.

> Firefighters use chainsaws to cut gaps in the forest to keep fires from spreading.

Instead of hoses, smokejumpers use hand tools and chainsaws to stop the fire. They cut a gap in the forest by cutting down fuel sources, such as bushes and trees. When they are finished, the jumpers carry their gear to the nearest road or helicopter landing spot.

9

Number of smokejumper bases in the US

- Smokejumpers may have science degrees in ecology, forestry, or biology.
- Many smokejumpers have over 10 seasons of firefighting experience.
- Smokejumpers also provide rescue and first-aid services to people in remote areas.

NEDS FOR LIFE

The McCall Smokejumper Base is located in McCall, Idaho. The base is used to train smokejumpers. New trainees are called *Neds*. In order to be a Ned, the trainee must already have at least 90 days of wildfire fighting experience.

2

Smokejumpers Parachute into Wildfires

After jumping out of a plane and guiding the parachute to earth, the smokejumper's real challenge begins.

Smokejumpers leave the airplane with their parachute gear. They also take safety equipment for the jump and some tools for firefighting. Most smokejumpers use ram-air parachutes. These parachutes are shaped like rectangles. They work well in areas with high winds.

After the smokejumpers jump out of the plane, the plane turns around. It makes a low pass over the smokejumpers. Chainsaws, sleeping bags, water, and other equipment are thrown from the plane. The equipment is also attached to parachutes. But sometimes these get stuck in trees. The smokejumpers have to climb the trees to get their gear.

A BIG RESPONSIBILITY

The spotter stays with the plane and the pilot. They choose a safe place where the smokejumpers will land. The spotter makes sure everyone leaves the plane safely. They provide the jumpers and the pilot with information. They tell them about the wind, the terrain, and the fire. They make sure the jumpers have everything they need for the next 72 hours.

More and more smokejumpers are women.

Smokejumpers Are Always Ready

Smokejumpers make certain their parachutes are in top condition.

When there are no fires, smokejumpers stay prepared. They pack cargo boxes. These boxes contain food and equipment for the smokejumpers to use on missions. One cargo box holds enough food and water for two smokejumpers. It can last for three or four days. Some cargo boxes hold other items, such as sleeping bags, tools, and first aid kits.

The smokejumpers also inspect their parachutes. They clean their equipment. They make sure their plane is stocked.

They never know when they might be called out to another fire.

When they are not fighting fires, smokejumpers receive medical training. Some become Emergency Medical Technicians (EMTs). That way, they can take care of injuries that might occur when parachuting or firefighting.

Fighting fires requires a lot of equipment and supplies.

THINK ABOUT IT

Have you prepared for a fire emergency at home or at school? What did you do?

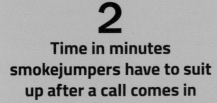

2

Time in minutes smokejumpers have to suit up after a call comes in

- Jumpers are ready to take off within 10 to 15 minutes.
- Their supplies include some of their favorite foods such as Gatorade and ramen noodles.
- They also carry glow sticks and emergency whistles so they can locate each other.

9

Smokejumpers Work as Teams

Fighting fires is a team effort.

Smokejumpers train to make sure they can survive on their own. But they fight fires in teams. Sometimes the jumpers put out the fire. Other times, they turn it over to another team.

The teams are tight-knit groups of men and women. The members of the team look out for each other. Each team has a foreman and squad leader. The leaders map out the fire before making the jump.

Smokejumpers must communicate well with other members of the team. They should be able to speak honestly

Team communication is essential to successfully complete plans.

with their leader and each other. Once on the ground, the foreman involves the team in making decisions. They talk about strategies and risks. They decide if the team is comfortable taking those risks. The best leaders listen to their team. Sometimes team members give the leader a better way to think about a problem.

Smokejumper teams take turns fighting fires.

20
Number of members on the largest smokejumper teams

- Teams may be made up of only two people.
- The size of the fire and availability of resources determines how many smokejumpers are called.
- Teams that just finished an assignment are placed at the bottom of a jump list. Those at the top will jump next.

11

The Smokejumper Program Began in 1939

Many early smokejumpers had no parachute experience.

The smokejumper program started as an experiment. It began in the US Pacific Northwest. Four men had experience jumping. Seven others had never jumped before. During training, they completed 60 jumps. By 1940, Washington had six smokejumpers, and Idaho had seven. Rufus Robinson from Idaho and Earl Cooley from Montana made the first jump into a real fire on July 12, 1940.

During World War II, the smokejumper program slowed down. But more bases were

PAVING THE WAY

Deanne Shulman became the first female smokejumper in 1979. Many thought women could not do the job physically. Shulman was strong enough. But she lost her position because she was underweight. Shulman filed a complaint, and the required weight was lowered. She was allowed to try again. She jumped for five years, beginning in 1981.

established, and a lot of inexperienced jumpers were trained. In 1944, the Forest Service officially took on the project, with 110 smokejumpers.

A spotter in the plane watches to make sure the jump was safe.

In 1945 the 555th Infantry Airborne African-American unit successfully put out several forest fires set by Japanese incendiary bombs.

9
Number of fires smokejumpers jumped into during their first year

- The first official jump was made into the Nez Perce Forest in Idaho.
- Lightning caused a record number of fires that year.
- The smokejumpers saved approximately $30,000 in damages.

Smokejumpers Must Be in Good Shape

Physical training is an important part of smokejumper preparation.

To be able to fight fires, smokejumpers must be physically fit. They need both strength and endurance. They have a lot of heavy equipment to carry through difficult terrain.

Smokejumpers must be in excellent condition even before they start training. They must be able to complete certain exercises in a set amount of time. If they can't, they can't become a smokejumper.

For example, trainees go to smokejumper bases for training. On the first day, they must be able to complete 7 pull-ups, 45 sit-ups, and 25 push-ups. They have to be

Smokejumper equipment is heavy.

able to run 1.5 miles (2.4 km) in less than 11 minutes. They must also be able to carry a 110-pound (50-kg) pack for three miles in 90 minutes or less. At some smokejumper bases, the requirements are even more difficult.

THINK ABOUT IT

What kind of exercises do you do to stay physically fit?

60

Number of sit-ups trainees have to do at the base in Alaska

- It takes weeks of training to get in shape.
- Smokejumpers are tested each year to make sure they can still fight fires effectively.
- They use a training routine to stay in shape when they are not working.

Smokejumpers Work for the Government

The US Forest Service is one of the organizations in charge of hiring smokejumpers. The smokejumper bases are located in Alaska, Idaho, California, Montana, Washington, and Oregon. But smokejumpers are considered a resource for the whole country. That means that any state can call on them for help. They fight wildfires all around the country.

The US Forest Service operated DC-3 aircraft for over 40 years, until retiring the last one in 2015.

Smokejumpers rely on the support of other team members.

Applicants must have already demonstrated firefighting skills. They must already know how to use hand tools, chainsaws, and portable pumps. After applying to work as a smokejumper, applicants must travel to a base and pass smokejumper training.

Most smokejumpers are temporary employees who work during the wildfire season. But some have permanent jobs. These are mostly supervisors, who work on equipment and training. Smokejumpers usually earn $16 an hour. But depending on the position, a foreman smokejumper can earn $24 per hour.

400
Number of smokejumpers in the United States

- Alaska had 63 smokejumpers.
- In July 2019, Alaska was dealing with a lot of wildfires in different areas. More than 140 smokejumpers from other states came to help.
- It set a record for the most smokejumpers in the state at one time.

Some Smokejumpers Work Seasonally

Wildfires are most common in the hot, dry months.

Some smokejumpers work only during wildfire season. This is the time when wildfires are most likely to occur. Wildfire season in the US used to be about four months long. Now, it can be six to eight months long. One reason is that the snow melts earlier in the winter. Also, rain comes later in the fall. Long periods

Today there are nearly 300 female smokejumpers in the US.

18
Minimum age required to become a smokejumper

- Most new smokejumpers are in their 20s.
- Some smokejumpers turn their seasonal job into a lifelong career.
- Smokejumpers must retire when they are 57 years old.

Others have jobs that give them extra time during the summer months. Some are students or teachers. Some work in the snow ski industry. But seasonal smokejumpers come from many other occupations. They may be construction workers or doctors. They might be lawyers or artists.

of drought can also affect the wildfire season.

Because smokejumpers don't work all year round, they have other jobs, too. Some work as regular firefighters.

THINK ABOUT IT

What are some jobs you could do during the summer?

Smokejumpers Need Special Equipment

The pulaski firefighting tool was invented in 1911 by Ed Pulaski, a US Forest Service ranger.

Smokejumpers work miles from civilization. Because of this, they don't have access to water and hoses. They take along portable water pumps. They also bring firefighting chemicals.

Because smokejumpers have to carry their tools, they use hand tools. In most situations, smokejumpers use chainsaws or pulaskis to fight the fire. A pulaski is a combination between an axe and a hoe. They use these tools to cut

Wildfires burn on average 1500°F (800°C).

and dig up anything the fire can use for fuel. They create a wide fireline or gap in the forest ground that won't burn. This fireline helps keep the fire from spreading.

16
Number of hours a smokejumper may be working on a fireline

- Smokejumpers carry a personal fire shelter.
- The fire shelter is a one-person tent made to resist heat.
- If the fire is moving too fast, the smokejumpers dig into the ground and get under the shelter.

ON ITS WAY

Sometimes smokejumpers need more equipment. Paracargo is cargo attached to parachutes. Food and tools are packed and loaded onto the plane. The pilots and spotters communicate with the jumpers on the ground. They drop the boxes over a certain location. The cargo floats to the ground, where the smokejumpers can collect it.

Rookie Training Is Tough

Hands-on training includes tree climbing and cutting with a chainsaw.

Smokejumpers come from fire crews across the US. First, they join a rookie training program to learn the skills they'll need to succeed. But not every trainee will become a smokejumper.

Trainees are evaluated on their ability to learn, their teamwork skills, and their firefighting skills. They must pass the physical training test on the first day. After that, they have physical training sessions every day. In class, they cover topics such

as steering a parachute and first aid.

Trainees also learn the basics of parachuting. Landings are unpredictable. But smokejumpers practice to make sure they are prepared for any situation. Bases have equipment that lets trainees know what jumping feels like. It lifts them up and drops them at speeds of up to 10 mph (16 kph). The trainees learn how to land safely without getting hurt.

Smokejumper medical training includes CPR techniques.

5

Number of weeks of training for new smokejumpers at the McCall base in Idaho

- Returning jumpers receive a two-week refresher course.
- They review parachuting and firefighting techniques.
- Returning smokejumpers also attend 8 to 24 hours of medical training every year.

Smokejumpers Make a Lot of Things They Use

Smokejumper jumpsuits feature a high, padded collar to protect their faces and necks from branches and other hard objects.

One of the skills smokejumpers learn is how to make and repair their own jumpsuits. The jumpsuits have special features. They are padded and made of Kevlar. Kevlar is a very strong material that can take a lot of heat. Lots of pockets hold items such as remote radios and hacking tools.

Smokejumpers make their own firefighter packs. They use the packs to carry the gear and supplies they will need.

MORE PROTECTION

The only equipment the jumpers don't make themselves are their jump helmets and parachutes. Their helmets are similar to motorcycle helmets. They have a cage-like face mask for protection. That way, tree branches and brush can't get in the smokejumper's eyes.

Smokejumpers also make their own parachute harnesses. They inspect and repair their parachutes. Because sewing is such an important part of smokejumping, bases have sewing rooms.

Because smokejumper suits and other gear are unique and cannot be bought in a store, individuals have to learn to make and repair things.

14
Number of sewing machines in the Smokejumper Parachute Loft

- The Loft is where smokejumpers in Redding, Washington sew.
- They spend their days sewing as they wait for a fire call.
- Some machines are specialized for heavy-duty work.

25

Smokejumpers May Hit the Ground Hard

A static line is attached to the aircraft and automatically opens the parachute once the jumper is safely away from the plane.

The first danger smokejumpers face is landing safely on the ground. Most smokejumpers land in rough terrain in mountain forests. It's important for smokejumpers to learn how to land correctly. If they don't, they could suffer from serious injuries.

Ram-air parachutes are designed to allow smokejumpers to steer and land where they aim.

When the signal is given, the smokejumpers leave the aircraft from a sitting position. When the parachutes open, the smokejumpers steer toward their landing zone. Sometimes smokejumpers aim for trees if there is no clearing. Once they are caught in a tree, they drop themselves to the ground with their safety line.

Most smokejumpers use ram-air parachutes. The smokejumpers are able to steer these parachutes. That way, they have more control of where they land. Smokejumpers also have a backup parachute. This parachute has an automatic device that starts to work if the jumper is unconscious.

1,500
Height in feet (457 m) at which smokejumpers leave the plane

- To land safely, smokejumpers try to hit the ground with both feet together.
- After touching the ground, they roll to one side.
- This technique is called a *parachute landing fall*.

More Daring and Dangerous Jobs

Aerial Firefighter Pilot

Aerial firefighter pilots are also known as air tanker pilots. They help fight wildfires. Their job is to drop fire-fighting chemicals from an airplane. While most work seasonally, the US Forest Service hires some full-time pilots.

Hotshot Firefighter

Hotshots work in the hottest part of a wildfire. They use many kinds of specialized hand tools, such as chainsaws and fireline explosives. Hotshots work in all phases of wildfire firefighting, from building firelines to making sure the fire has burned out.

Helitack Crew Member

A helitack crew member is a firefighter who is transported by helicopter to the wildfire. Helicopters provide quick transport. Once at the fire, the crew assesses the situation. They use hand tools to build firelines. They often stay at the location overnight.

Glossary

applicant
A person who completes the necessary paperwork to get a certain job.

drought
A long period of time with little or no rain.

endurance
The ability to continue doing something that is tiring or hard.

foreman
A worker who supervises and directs other workers.

portable
Something that is easy to carry or move such as small, light equipment.

rookie
Someone without experience who has just started doing a job.

suppress
To put out a fire or prevent it from growing.

terrain
The physical features of the land, such as hills, rocks, and mountains.

trainee
Someone who is learning how to do a certain job or profession.

tight-knit
A group of people bound together by strong relationships.

underweight
Weight that is below the amount required.

Thiessen, Mark. *Extreme Wildfire: Smoke Jumpers, High-Tech Gear, Survival Tactics, and the Extraordinary Science of Fire.* Washington, DC: National Geographic Children's Books, 2016

Westmark, Jon. *Smoke Jumpers in Action (Dangerous Jobs in Action).* North Mankato, MN: The Child's World, 2017

Maurer, Tracy Nelson. *The World's Worst Wildfires (World's Worst Natural Disasters).* North Mankato, MN: Capstone Press, 2019

Visit 12StoryLibrary.com

Scan the code or use your school's login at **12StoryLibrary.com** for recent updates about this topic and a full digital version of this book. Enjoy free access to:

- Digital ebook
- Breaking news updates
- Live content feeds
- Videos, interactive maps, and graphics
- Additional web resources

Note to educators: Visit 12StoryLibrary.com/register to sign up for free premium website access. Enjoy live content plus a full digital version of every 12-Story Library book you own for every student at your school.

Index

About the Author

Samantha S. Bell has written more than 125 nonfiction books for children. She also teaches art and creative writing to children and adults. She lives in the Carolinas with her family and too many cats.